300 things I hope

written by IAIN S. THOMAS

illustrated by CARLA KREUSER

central
avenue
publishing

2016

Published by Central Avenue Publishing, an imprint of Central Avenue Marketing Ltd.
www.centralavenuepublishing.com

Published in Canada
Printed in United States of America

1. SELF HELP / Motivational & Inspirational 2. POETRY / General

Library and Archives Canada Cataloguing in Publication

Thomas, Iain S., author
        300 things I hope / Iain S. Thomas ; illustrated by Carla Kreuser.

Poems.
Issued in print and electronic formats.
ISBN 978-1-77168-046-2 (paperback).--ISBN 978-1-77168-047-9 (epub).--
ISBN 978-1-77168-048-6 (mobi)

        I. Kreuser, Carla, illustrator II. Title. III. Title: Three hundred
things I hope.
PR9369.4.T56A613 2016   821'.92   C2016-902757-0
                                                        C2016-902758-9

For Evelyn
You are my heart
— Iain

For Hudson & Finley
xx
— Carla

1

I hope someone gives you this book
or you find it at a time when you need it.

2

I hope you've found or will find love.

3

I hope you find a stranger to whisper you to sleep.

4

I hope people love you when you're born and as long as you live.

5

I hope you love someone like the
solar system loves the sun.

6

I hope you learn everything you need to learn
before what you don't learn, hurts you.

7

I hope you never become something you hate.

8

I hope you have the courage to do things for the first time.

9

I hope you don't wait too long to do them.

10

I hope you always have a pen.

11

I hope you're proud of every difficult thing you do.

12

I hope you never have a sleepless night.

13

I hope a doctor never looks at you seriously and says,

"It's not good."

14

I hope you always have something
to say in a lift.

15

I hope you meet someone who's as close to your soulmate as possible while actually being real.

16

I hope someone famous retweets you.

17

I hope you're never disappointed when
you meet someone famous.

18

I hope you become famous and people want to meet you.

19

I hope you never forget who you
once were.

20

I hope you are never forgotten.

21

I hope you love whenever you're given the chance to love.

22

I hope you never hate anything longer than you need to.

23

I hope you have the energy and the drive
to keep doing things until you succeed.

24

I hope you know there's no overnight success.

25

I hope you experience a runner's high and never stop running.

26

I hope you love your family.

27

I hope you having nothing to say to them when they pass on to the next world, and that you've said everything you need to.

28

I hope you have a friend you stay friends with forever.

29

I hope you die holding hands with someone you love.

30

I hope you die knowing that there was no end to the road,
and that the road was all there ever was,
and that all that mattered was how well you walked
each individual step of it.

31

I hope you take pictures of the things you love.

32

I hope no one deletes them by mistake.

33

I hope you are tagged in every photo.

34

I hope that if love hurts, it teaches you something about yourself or about someone else.

35

I hope nothing, ever, hurts.

36

I hope that everything eventually means something.

37

I hope you work hard at making yourself who you want to be.

38

I hope you discover a book written entirely about you.

39

I hope there's a kind of fire that only you know.

40

I hope you get to meet aliens or your favourite band.

41

I hope you get to meet yourself as a stranger.

42

I hope you find truth at the top of the bottle
and not at the bottom of it.

43

I hope you never lose something that cannot be found.

44

I hope you never lose.

45

I hope you get the respect you deserve and
I hope you give it, too.

46

I hope you wake up, look in the mirror,
and like the person who looks back at you.

47

I hope you invent something really simple
that makes you a lot of money.

48

I hope you never have to think
about money, ever.

49

I hope you discover how much more there is to being happy.

50

I hope you know that nothing gets done in a day.
Most things take two.

51

I hope the person you love runs their fingers along
your back when you sleep.

52

I hope they can sculpt you in their dreams.

53

I hope nothing changes.

54

I hope everything changes.

55

I hope you invent rules for yourself if you don't have any.

56

I hope you break them if you already do.

57

I hope everyone who touches you has the softest, gentlest hands.

58

I hope every tear you ever cry
makes you feel a little bit better.

59

I hope you never lose your shoes and if you do,
I hope you find better ones and I hope they fit, perfectly.

60

I hope you're never in a position that
forces you to steal shoes.

61

I hope the only thing you're ever hungry for is more life.

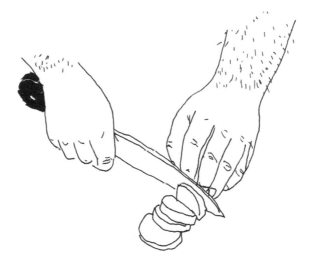

62

I hope you never sit next to someone in a movie who tells you what's about to happen before it happens.

63

I hope you earn all the trust
you're given.

64

I hope the person who loves you has many reasons for doing so, all of them noble and good.

65

I hope you are touched by the smallest gestures of friendship.

66

I hope you forgive.

67

I hope you are forgiven.

68

I hope you discover what it's like to lose an argument
and be ok with it.

69

I hope you feel everything you're supposed to feel,
when you're supposed to feel it.

70

I hope you live a long life.

71

I hope you always feel young while you live it.

72

I hope your shoelaces never come undone.

73

I hope your hair never gets wet
when you don't want it to be.

74

I hope someone kisses you when you least expect it.

75

I hope you learn to love yourself.

76

I hope you never consider caring for yourself indulgent.

77

I hope you are never hated for what you look like,
sound like, or where you believe we all come from.

78

I hope you never hate others for those same reasons.

79

I hope you compose symphonies in your head
when you're alone.

80

I hope those symphonies bring you great success.

81

I hope you inspire other people to compose symphonies,
too.

82

I hope you learn the difference between the easy thing,
the hard thing, the smart thing and the right thing.

83

I hope you never believe something because you're too afraid not to.

84

I hope love moves through your heart like
light moves through glass.

85

I hope you're on a hidden camera show, and everyone you thought hated you jumps out of cupboards to tell you they love you.

86

I hope you have catnip or a fish with you
every time you meet a cat.

87

I hope you have a cat with you every time you meet a dog.

88

I hope you forget every embarrassing thing
that's ever happened to you.

89

I hope you run like the wind
and the air itself carries you forward.

90

I hope you have a favourite song from your favourite band
and that song plays on your wedding day.

91

I hope someone always laughs at your jokes,
even if it's you.

92

I hope you carry on.

93

I hope you find beautiful things in simple things.

94

I hope you remember that everything leaves a mark,
which is a double-edged sword.
The marks are beautiful and the marks are scars,
and both cut you out of the universe,
define you and make you, you.

95

I hope you discover that love is both a feeling and an action, like light is both a particle and a wave.

96

I hope that if you find a genie who grants three wishes,
he gives you four.

97

I hope you use that fourth wish on something involving ice cream.

98

I hope the Earth is around for
at least as long as you are.

99

I hope your plants always grow.

100

I hope that if your life ever goes off track, that one day you wake up and decide to change everything.

101

I hope that any noise you hear in the night is only someone you love coming home.

102

I hope everyone cries at your funeral.

103

I hope you do things worthy of those tears.

104

I hope you reach beyond yourself,
constantly.

105

I hope you grasp the universe and that it tingles.

106

I hope you write a sublime concept album that nobody understands but everybody loves.

107

I hope you get up and clean everything around you and that it feels like a fresh start.

108

I hope you drink enough coffee to get you out of bed
but not so much that you can't find your way back there.

109

I hope you have the strength to make something difficult seem easy, because that's grace and it's important.

110

I hope you never get angry enough to be stupid or stupid enough to be angry.

111

I hope when it rains, you are
near a window.

112

I hope you are your own person.

113

I hope you're kind.

114

I hope your phone rings now and it's someone you desperately want to hear from.

115

I hope your earphones are comfortable.

116

I hope you love the sun or that the sun still loves you,
even if you don't.

Even if you just love it in secret.

117

I hope that stupid people
never break your heart.

118

I hope your heart is made of something hard and soft at the same time.

119

I hope you see something everyone's seen a million times,
and you see something different.

120

I hope you have great parents, a great parent or someone
who became like a great parent to you.

121

I hope you become something similar one day
to someone else.

122

I hope you build your world
one grain of sand at a time.

123

I hope when you give a gift, you know that the value of it is only what it cost you to give.

124

I hope your clothes fit the same at home
as they did at the store.

125

I hope when you put them on and a song starts to play, you're inspired to do great things and everything feels like a really cool music video, starring you.

126

I hope the coffee is never cold when it touches your lips.

127

I hope the food is always warm
on the end of your fork.

128

I hope you always have enough and never too much.

129

I hope the only time you compare yourself to someone else is when you ask yourself how you'd feel if you were them.

130

I hope you respect everyone who does little things for you.

131

I hope you do little things for others.

132

I hope your watch is always right, except when being late for something saves your life or being early changes your life for the better.

133

I hope that sometimes you just know things and
find yourself in love with a person
who wants you to know them.

134

I hope you do hard things when you're given the chance to do them and you're never afraid to do them.

135

I hope your computer never crashes.

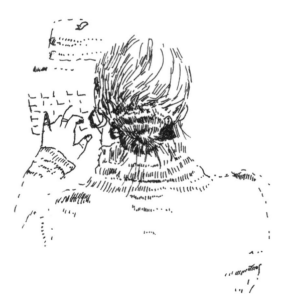

136

I hope you know that dreaming a dream is not the same as making something happen.

137

I hope it feels like your muscles are singing when you exercise.

138

I hope you're in a meeting one day and no one's talking
and then you think of something really funny to say,
and you say it.

139

I hope you never listen to anyone who tells you that
you can't sing, dance, write or paint.

140

I hope one day you develop a one-person art experience
that involves you singing, dancing, writing and painting,
all at the same time.

141

I hope the tickets to it sell out.

142

I hope you never feel like you're falling apart.

143

I hope that if you ever do actually fall apart, you only ever lose the pieces of yourself you didn't want anymore.

144

I hope that if something bad happens to you,
that the world suddenly starts turning backwards and it
unhappens to you.

145

I hope there is always someone
next to you when you cry.

146

I hope you have the courage to stay next to someone
when they cry.

147

I hope you come up with a really interesting theory regarding where we all go when we die, and you're right.

148

I hope you're brave enough to be what you need to be,
when you need to be it.

149

I hope you're kind and gentle
with yourself.

150

I hope that if you ever have a job that requires you to serve
people for several hours a day,
that everyone you serve is kind to you.

151

I hope you're never so proud of doing things on your own, of being alone, that you give a friend away like they mean nothing to you, just to prove a point.

152

I hope you're never lonely.

153

I hope you're never lonely.

154

I hope you're never lonely.

155

I hope you never feel like you're drifting through time.

156

I hope you notice little changes.

157

I hope your sunglasses never get scratched.

158

I hope every kitchen appliance you ever use works.

159

I hope the worst thing that ever breaks is a toaster.

160

I hope you spend a day on a train.

161

I hope you find something unexplainable on
the side of a road, like it was left there just for you.

162

I hope you experience a moment of truth and beauty that inspires you for years and sets your eyes on fire, and that everyone who looks at you after that moment knows that you have changed.

163

I hope if you ever have to give a presentation,
it is about the shape and the size of your heart, or kittens.

164

I hope everyone stands up and claps when you're done.

165

I hope you take short breaks
between things.

166

I hope you think big thoughts when you look at the stars.

167

I hope you find things that make you feel both small and big at the same time.

168

I hope you discover the freedom that exists beyond
despair, when you realise how little everything matters.

169

I hope if you ever propose or someone proposes to you, that the ring is made of the heart of something ancient and magical.

170

I hope you find time to sit in
a bay window and read.

171

I hope you overhear a conversation about yourself and everything they say is good.

172

I hope you say kind things about yourself in your head.

173

I hope you're brave enough to grab your own wrists if you beat yourself up, and whisper in your own ear, "Stop."

174

I hope you're brave enough to hug yourself and be ok with yourself as everyone else will go away eventually but you will always have to live with you.

175

I hope you give yourself presents.

176

I hope you never try and fill the emptiness inside with anything but love.

177

I hope you take long drives on your own.

178

I hope you love clouds as much as you love the sun.

179

I hope when it's cold, you always remember a jacket.

180

I hope the sunrise fills you with a sense of wonder
at its promise.

181

I hope you put on a one-act play in front of a security camera at a shopping mall.

182

I hope you look beautiful when you sleep.

183

I hope nothing you ever search for on a web browser comes back to haunt you.

184

I hope every act you commit
is a true expression of who you are.

185

I hope one day you're looking at the stars, and one shoots.

186

I hope a stranger says something that changes your entire day.

187

I hope you wear your heart on your sleeve.

188

I hope you don't make a habit of wearing a jacket made of heartache and hearts.

189

I hope you learn the difference between someone in a bad mood and a negative influence on your life.

190

I hope you're never hurt more than you can stand.

191

I hope you have the courage and strength of spirit to recognise when someone else is right.

192

I hope you have the strength of character to recognise when you're right.

193

I hope you get to relax when you retire
and plan accordingly.

194

I hope you keep yourself incredibly busy until then and that each day, you wake up with a new plan to conquer the world.

195

I hope you're determined when you need to be,
in the little moments of life that make it easy to give up.

196

I hope you never give up.

197

I hope you learn the difference between giving up and changing direction.

198

I hope you take your shoes off one day and there's a really soft carpet under your feet.

199

I hope a cat sleeps on your lap.

200

I hope a dog licks your hand.

201

I hope a bird never, ever, ever does its business on you.

202

I hope you learn to skate.

203

I hope you drive a nice car.

204

I hope you live in a nice house.

205

I hope you know that when I say "nice" I don't mean expensive, I mean I hope what you own makes you happy, it doesn't have to be a lot.

206

I hope you constantly search the world for more but you're always satisfied with what you have.

207

I hope you learn to balance what you need
and what you want.

208

I hope you cover something
in stickers.

209

I hope you carve the name of someone important into something important to you.

210

I hope your name is carved somewhere important.

211

I hope you write a message, put it in a bottle
and throw it into the sea.

212

I hope it's a secret and that someone,
somewhere, knows it.

213

I hope you are someone's secret and that somewhere in
the ocean, there's a bottle with your name in it.

214

I hope you look up at the sky at night and wonder if there's someone exactly like you living on another planet.

215

I hope you love the way the fire lights up someone's face.

216

I hope you jump into a pool and breathe all the air out of
your lungs just to know what it feels like
to sink to the bottom.

217

I hope you always remember to swim back up,
from anything.

218

I hope you take big gulps of air when you break the surface and the noise in the air and the water washes over you and it's amazing to feel alive.

219

I hope that you splash people and
that people splash you.

220

I hope you jump from the highest diving board.

221

I hope the sun shines but you never get a sunburn.

222

I hope life unravels beautifully, like tape from a roll.

223

I hope each day is better than the last.

224

I hope you have nights filled with fireworks and parties.

225

I hope you have nights filled with warm fires and blankets.

226

I hope you read the books you love reading and that reading never feels like hard work.

227

I hope you get driven around in a convertible and you put your hands in the air.

228

I hope the wind against your skin feels like the raw edge of life.

229

I hope you never sell who you could be
to become a safe nobody.

230

I hope you love yourself and you're kind to yourself whenever you need to be.

231

I hope you're kind.

232

I hope you drink enough water.

233

I hope you sometimes wonder if water is only tasteless
because we drink so much of it and maybe there's
something out there in space that aliens drink
that tastes like lemonade.

I hope you stay
a child forever.

235

I hope that you find something to do that moves you
gracefully through each day.

236

I hope you do something brave in an emergency and afterwards, as you're walking away, everyone claps.

237

I hope whenever you see someone less fortunate than
yourself, you see yourself in their eyes
and the life you could've had.

238

I hope you're good for the world.

239

I hope people say "the world is a poorer place" after you're gone.

240

I hope you never fear death because you know
you lived each day to its fullest.

241

I hope you go somewhere nice that only you know about
and you go there often.

242

I hope you always get what you deserve
and that what you deserve, is love.

243

I hope after a fight, you go over it in your head, and apologise for the things you didn't mean.

244

I hope you do this even if the other person doesn't, but they probably will and if they don't, then I hope you know you're a better person than they are.

245

I hope you never struggle to find a toothpick
when you need one.

246

I hope people get you blank books for Christmas every year because you're always filling them with ideas.

247

I hope you love the shapes
you see in clouds.

248

I hope you love little things.

249

I hope you know whatever you need to know without ever thinking you know everything.

250

I hope there's always some mystery left somewhere.

251

I hope there's a certain kind of joy you find in a heavy piano key and the sound it makes when you push it down.

252

I hope someone plays a song on a guitar for you and
the song they're playing is about you and
how wonderful you are.

253

I hope you learn to play something,
even if it's the tambourine.

254

I hope you're ok with playing the triangle, too.

255

I hope you sing to yourself softly sometimes.

256

I hope you sing loudly in the shower and
don't care who hears you.

257

I hope you hear a song on the radio and decide that it's
yours and take ownership of it like
you're planting a flag on a foreign land.

258

I hope that if someone stops to help you change a tyre,
they're about as far from a serial killer as you can get.

259

I hope you always fight about little things with someone
before they have the chance to become big things.

260

I hope you never ride over a cable with a chair and ruin it and cry. It's just a thing, we all make mistakes and everything will be ok.

261

I hope your doorbell plays a silly song and you laugh every time someone presses it.

262

I hope they laugh too.

263

I hope it isn't someone serious at the door,
like a policeman.

264

I hope it's the pizza guy and it's a surprise.

265

I hope you never stop appreciating surprise pizza.

266

I hope you never stop appreciating anything.

267

I hope you see Halley's Comet.

268

I hope medicine advances at a terrific rate and you see Halley's Comet a bunch of times.

269

I hope you spend the day in a rowboat and at night when you're falling asleep, you have the sensation of floating.

270

I hope you don't get seasick.

271

I hope you look out the window of a plane and wonder at all the people below you.

272

I hope you realise when you're on the ground, how many people are doing that above you.

273

I hope someone yawns near you and then you yawn.

274

I hope that yawn came from another yawn that came from
another yawn that came from someone you love.

275

I hope the exact same thing happens with a smile.

276

I hope this makes you think of how far a smile can travel.

277

I hope you're always brave and know that the only time you can be brave is when you're really afraid.

278

I hope you're never too polite to demand the life you want from the world around you.

279

I hope you're always polite enough
to be invited back somewhere.

280

I hope if things are going badly,
that you wake up and it was all a dream.

281

I hope if you do have dreams about your life,
that they're amazing dreams.

282

I hope they're never as good as how absolutely amazing
your life and all its potential really is.

283

I hope if your phone rings in the middle of the night,
it's emergency good news, not bad.

284

I hope if it is bad, that you and the other person on the line
are there for each other and that's why they phoned you.

285

I hope if you're climbing a cliff,
that you can always find the next thing to grab onto.

286

I hope you don't live like you're climbing a cliff.

287

I hope you live like you're walking in a forest.

288

I hope you pick things up as you go and
leave behind what you no longer need.

289

I hope you travel through life lightly.

290

I hope dappled sunlight follows you
through the rest of your days.

291

I hope your path intersects many others.

292

I hope you stop next to a waterfall to rest and you hear voices in the sound of the water.

293

I hope they always say nice things.

294

I hope moss grows on the stones at your feet.

295

I hope squirrels cheer you on, as you go.

296

I hope crickets chirp
as the sun sets.

297

I hope you climb a mountain to watch the colours change.

298

I hope you look around you and are filled with peace.

299

I hope you close your eyes
as you close this book.

300

I, honestly and truly, hope you're well.

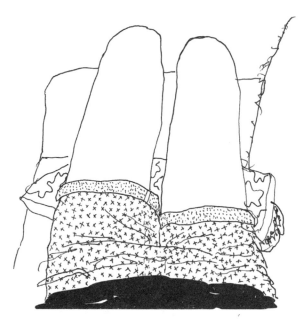

About Iain:

Iain S. Thomas is a new media artist and author. As an author, his most famous work is I Wrote This For You, a blog then book that's been on poetry bestseller lists since its launch in 2011. He regularly writes for The Huffington Post on poetry, creativity and life and currently lives in Cape Town, South Africa.

iainsthomas.com

About Carla:

Carla Kreuser is a graphic designer, and sometimes poet, with a penchant for horror stories and binding her own illustrated books by hand. She grew up in Pretoria, South Africa but currently lives closer to the sea in Cape Town, where she met poet Iain Thomas. In her spare time, she fills her sketchbooks by exploring the city on foot and people-watching.

carlakreuser.co.za

Other Books by Iain S. Thomas

I Wrote This For You is the first collection of the best photography and prose of the world-renowned blog, I Wrote This For You, from 2007 to 2011. Discover the blog at iwrotethisforyou.me

I Wrote This For You And Only You is the second collection from the *I Wrote This For You* project, it contains all the best photography and prose from 2011 to 2015.

I Wrote This For You: Just The Words was published in 2013 and contains 400 of the best poems from *I Wrote This For You* blog but only select photography.

Intentional Dissonance is a science fiction novel about Jon Salt, a young man in a dark dystopian future, addicted to a drug that causes sadness and unable to control his gift that turns his thoughts into reality.

25 Love Poems For The NSA was created in response to the information exposed by Edward Snowden, this short ebook contains 25 poems created using words that the NSA flags and tracks in email communication.

I Am Incomplete Without You is a collection of prompts and creative questions designed to inspire and provoke poetry in the reader, who then becomes the writer. Read excerpts and responses at iamincompletewithoutyou.com

How To Be Happy: Not A Self-Help Book. Seriously. is a collection of poetry, prose and short stories set within the story of the author's desperate attempt to write a self-help book about being happy.

iainsthomas.com